DO YOU KNOW
WHERE THE
ANIMALS
LIVE?

DO YOU KNOW WHERE THE ANIMALS LIVE?

DISCOVERING THE INCREDIBLE CREATURES ALL AROUND US

PETER WOHLLEBEN

Translated by
SHELLEY TANAKA

GREYSTONE KIDS
GREYSTONE BOOKS · VANCOUVER/BERKELEY

CONTENTS

LET'S GO ON A JOURNEY OF DISCOVERY

I'VE KEPT ANIMALS OF ALL KINDS ever since I was a kid. In my room I had a Mason jar full of mealworms that pupated and turned into black beetles. Once I used my grandmother's heating pad to hatch a chicken egg and see whether the chick would accept me as its mother. (It did!)

I've always spent a lot of time out and about in nature. I've croaked along with frogs and sniffed out the smell of wild boars in the forest. Later, when I became a forester, I observed animals every day.

Today, chickens, goats, horses, and dogs live with me and my wife, Miriam, at our forester's lodge. They've taught me a lot, such as how animal language works.

Animals have always been very important to me. And because I find them so interesting, I give regular guided tours of the woodland that I manage in the Eifel region of Western Germany.

Not everyone can visit me here in Europe. That's why I wrote this book, to tell you about the many animals I've seen both at my home and in my travels. From time to time I'll also take a look at animals that live farther away, such as in the ocean. There are many exciting things to report from there, too.

But much of what you'll read about here are things you can spot right outside your door or on a walk. There are also things you can observe and try out, either on your own, with your parents, or with friends. Maybe you'll even feel like answering a few quiz questions!

You'll find out what's going on in the hidden, exciting, dangerous, and funny world of animals. Do you know why it's a good thing that birds lay eggs, or that fish use farts to communicate? I'll also tell you why earthworms are afraid of the rain, how crows annoy dogs, and what you'll need to build a butterfly spa in your backyard.

Writing a book about animals has been great fun. But I couldn't have done it alone. On a very hot day last summer, Marit, Henrik, Mia, Ludwig, Romy, Justus, and Elias came to my place. Together we found animal tracks, visited animals, and tried out activities. Jens Steingässer, the photographer, took a lot of pictures. I discussed what should go in the book with Anja Fischer and Jane Billinghurst. They also helped make sure I didn't forget to include anything important. For this English edition of the book, Antonia Banyard helped select some new photographs, and Belle Wuthrich drew the illustrations and put the text, photographs, and illustrations together so that everything looked good, and Shelley Tanaka translated it from German so you could read it.

Now we're all set, so let's discover the world of animals together!

In this book, I'll show you how to experiment, build, and investigate things at home or outdoors. But you should always take an adult with you, especially if you are using power tools. You should never put anything in your mouth unless an adult can identify what it is, as some plants can be poisonous. If you have food allergies, it's best to avoid forest snacks altogether. And always remember not to touch any animals you're studying.

There is so much
to see in a pond.

CHAPTER 1

WHERE ANIMALS LIVE

YOU DON'T NEED TO GO TO A ZOO to see animals. You can look out a window and see robins flying by, take a walk in the woods to search for tracks and dens, or crouch down by a pond in a city park to search for tiny frogs. Animals are everywhere if you know where to look.

WHO LIVES IN YOUR BACKYARD?

Animals make themselves at home in many backyards. They especially like messy ones, where they can find shelter and enough to eat.

MOST ANIMALS ARE SHY, particularly large animals. That's why it's easier to watch small creatures. They'll sometimes spend their whole lives in the same yard, and they can't run away as fast as big animals.

*

Take ants, for example. They crawl around almost every lawn and path, building their nests in the ground, under rocks or dead wood. On the surface you'll just see very fine crumbs, like a mini molehill. Pay close attention, though, because the little red ants can bite. They're not dangerous, but their bites will burn like the touch of nettles. Ants are related to bees, and you already know how they can sting!

*

Other animals can be unpleasant to touch. After it rains, you may suddenly see slimy slugs in the flower beds. Of course, they have always lived there, but they usually hide under leaves and stones in good weather. They dry out quickly in the sun, because they have no shell to protect them, and they only dare to come out when it's wet and damp.

*

Winter is an especially good time for bird-watching, because most of the trees and shrubs have no leaves. You can sit by your window and watch birds such as

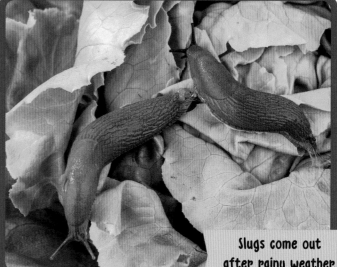

Slugs come out after rainy weather.

chickadees and robins feeding. During this time they can't find as much to eat in the woods and fields, so it's a good idea to set up a bird feeder.

Birds don't just get hungry, they also get thirsty. Most people forget this in the winter. When everything is frozen, the birds can no longer drink from puddles or small backyard ponds. They'll be happy if you set out a bowl of warm water every day. They like to take baths, too, even when it's cold out!

*

In the spring, many birds will look for a hollow to build a nest, where cats or squirrels can't get to their eggs and chicks. And because it can be hard for them to find hollows in suburban backyards, it's nice when people hang up nesting boxes. Each box has a hole that the bird can slip through. Different species of birds will nest in the box, depending on how big the hole is. Chickadees need a hole with a diameter of one and one-eighth inches (28 mm). They'll also move into boxes with bigger holes, but then larger birds may come in and chase them away. White-breasted nut-hatches (noisy little birds with clear black, white, and gray markings) will fit through holes that are at least one and one-quarter inches (32 mm) wide. Larger birds need even bigger entrances. So if you hang boxes with different-sized holes, you may see several species of breeding birds.

TRY THIS!

BUTTERFLIES GET HOT WHEN the sun shines, just as you do. You might sit under a tree or run through a lawn sprinkler to cool down. Butterflies look for moist sandy or muddy areas, where they fold up their wings to keep the sun from shining on them and sip the minerals they need to stay healthy. You can create a butterfly spa in your backyard by installing a water mister in a shady spot where there is bare soil, sand, or gravel. Every once in a while, you can add some rotting fruit as a special treat for the butterflies.

Look!

Ant Waste

DO YOU HAVE FORGET-ME-NOTS in your garden? If so, you may have noticed that they flower in new spots every year. Forget-me-not seeds have tiny packets of food attached to them that taste good to ants. The ants collect the seeds and take them to their burrows. Then they nibble on the food packets and deposit the seeds outside again as waste. The following year, forget-me-nots will bloom on these mounds of ant waste.

A messy pile of stones makes an excellent home for many animals.

WHY DO BIRDS FLY SOUTH?

Many animals have a permanent home for only a few weeks or months each year. This includes most species of birds. In the spring, birds look for a nice spot to build their nest.

ONCE BIRDS HAVE FINISHED building their nests, they will stay until their chicks are grown. Otherwise they'd have to carry their nest and chicks around with them! When the breeding season is over, and the chicks have left the nest, the birds give up their territories.

Even though each bird can now fly wherever it wants without entering another bird's territory, many robins, for instance, get so used to the cities and backyards where they've nested that they'll stay year round. And they'll defend their territories to do so, too. If a new robin comes flying in, the territory owner will chase it away. It won't be a serious attack, though the stranger may lose a feather or two.

Whose garden is this? Two male robins argue about it.

*

Other species will just fly off to where the food is in fall. Large flocks of birds may gather on branches near the berries and nuts that can be found on hedges between fields or at the edge of the forest. You may see small seedpods fluttering to the ground beneath a stand of birch trees. If you look up, there might be chickadees nibbling on the catkins dangling from the branches. Once they've eaten all the seeds, they can just fly to another birch forest. When you're hungry, it can be quite convenient not to have a permanent home!

*

Many birds in the Northern Hemisphere fly south as it turns cold in fall. The deciduous trees lose their leaves, the grass in the meadows turns brown or yellow, and most insects that don't die or migrate hide themselves away from the cold. Insects are important food for many birds, which now have to spend lots of time looking for them.

Fall storms are no fun if you have to fly against them. Birds may wait for a strong wind from the north so they can rise up into the air and be carried south. It's

Canada geese fly south in a distinctive V formation. If they are close, you might even hear them honking.

Look!

Hummingbirds

much more comfortable than flying into the wind. You may already know this from riding your bike. It's not as much fun when there's a strong wind blowing into your face, because you have to pedal much harder.

＊

Once they arrive in the south, the birds warm themselves in the sun and look for food. They'll fly to different countries, depending on what they like to eat. Where I live, for instance, cranes head for the oak forests of northern Spain in winter to eat all the acorns lying on the ground. In North America, you might see Canada geese flying south to find better sources of food.

＊

If you suddenly spot large flocks of migratory birds flying south in the fall, it may turn quite cold over the next few days. The birds are being carried on a wind blowing from the north, where it's already winter.

In the spring things work the other way around. When large flocks are carried back north on a southerly wind, a few warm days may be on the way. Warm air is carried by the wind from warmer, more southerly countries to more northerly countries.

HUMMINGBIRDS WEIGH LESS THAN a nickel (or, if you live in the UK, a 1p coin), but they are fearless fliers. They follow the spring bloom of their favorite flowers north and return to the same backyard feeders year after year. The longest hummingbird migration is three thousand miles (nearly 5,000 km). Some hummingbirds fly from Alaska, where they nest, to Mexico, where they eat insects in the winter. Others fly across the Gulf of Mexico, a five-hundred-mile (800-km), nonstop journey that takes them eighteen to twenty-two hours.

DO ANIMALS HAVE HOUSES?

Do animals need home addresses? They may not put up a sign with a house number on it, but there are animals that spend their whole lives living in one place.

Wolf pups stay safe in their den—from the weather, but also from predators like mountain lions or bears, which sometimes hunt young wolves.

A WOLF FAMILY LIVES in a very large permanent home—a territory of fifty to a thousand square miles (130 to 2,500 sq. km) depending on how large the pack is and how easy it is for them to find food. The wolves mark the borders of their territory with pee and scratch marks, so that every outsider wolf knows that area is occupied. Within these territories the wolves also have a house complete with a roof. They dig a deep den in the ground—that's where their pups come into the world.

Like wolves, mice prefer to live in families. And they have territories, too, but much smaller ones, because mice can't run very far. So their territory measures about a thousand square feet (100 sq. m)—about the size of a small house. You can walk across a mouse's territory in about fifteen steps. But you would need several hours to drive across a large wolf territory.

Just like wolves, mice dig deep burrows. The burrow is the mouse family's permanent home. The sleeping chamber is nicely padded with grass and moss to give the mice a dry, comfortable place to lie down and settle in.

*

Some animal homes are a little more, well, disgusting. Take the tapeworm, for example. They live inside the intestines of large animals such as fox and deer, and they live off whatever that particular animal eats. It's always nice and dark, damp, and warm in there, and the worm doesn't have to worry about a thing. When a deer eats something, the food comes through its stomach and intestine right to the happy worm. Because the worm eats up a lot of what's in its stomach, the deer is often hungry.

*

A permanent home is especially important to honeybees. They live in wooden boxes that beekeepers set up for them. There they raise their offspring in honeycombs. On one side of the box there's a small gap where they can fly in and out. But if you move the hive just a little bit to one side, the bees can no longer find the entrance. They just fly back to where it used to be. Out in nature, this doesn't happen because honeybees like to build their honeycombs inside hollow trees, which usually stay in one place.

Bees don't have territories like wolves. Once they've flown out of the hive, they're happy to share the meadows and forests with bees from other colonies.

Honeybees don't always stay in the same hive for their whole lives. Sometimes they move house. When a young queen hatches in the colony, the old one gathers some of her workers around her and flies away. Two queens in one hive won't do! The old queen and her part of the bee colony will look for a new home somewhere else, preferably in a hollow tree.

QUIZ

We have hundreds of species of bees. How do most of them live?

* All alone
* In colonies of two hundred
* In colonies of fifty thousand

Most bees do not live in colonies, they live completely alone. The honeybee with its big colonies is an exception.

Can you tell which animal has just walked by here?

EVEN IF YOU DON'T see the animals that live near you, you might see their tracks, and you can take these home with you. You'll need a bag of plaster (preferably the kind that hardens quickly), a yogurt container, and a little water. Mix the plaster powder with the water in the container until there are no lumps. Then pour the plaster into the footprint and wait until it hardens. Instructions on the package will tell you how long this takes. Finally, lift the plaster cast out and you're done! Be careful, because the cast can break easily. At home you can use an old toothbrush to brush off any soil. Check the internet to find out whose footprint you've captured.

WHAT CAN YOU FIND IN A STREAM?

It's not so easy to see animals in the water. That's because they're usually hiding, particularly from birds.

SOME BIRDS, LIKE PELICANS and herons, have big beaks for catching fish. Smaller birds like dippers have tiny beaks to pry out crustaceans or fly larvae that live under rocks in streams. So that's exactly where you can go to find them. Sit on the bank of a stream and lift a rock out of the water. On the underside you may see brown animals with two feelers sticking out at the back. These are the nymphs of stone flies. It's a good sign if you find them, because stone fly nymphs need very clean running water.

*

You may see small tubes moving between the stones in the water. They belong to the larvae of the caddis fly. To protect themselves from enemies, the larvae build themselves little cases. They'll glue together a tube out of tiny pebbles or plant parts, depending on what they find lying in the water.

*

You'll even find animals living in small pools of standing water, where frogs and toads may lay their eggs in March. The common frog lays its eggs in large clumps containing more than a thousand eggs. They swell up after being laid—otherwise they wouldn't all fit in the mother frog's belly! Tadpoles hatch from the eggs. They look like bullets with tails. Their favorite food is algae— tiny plants that grow like a green film on the surface and around the edges of the water.

In the summer, the tadpole's tail becomes shorter and shorter, and legs form on the sides of the body. After this, it won't be long before many tiny frogs and toads crawl out of the water.

Tadpoles often cluster together in shallow water.

Common mergansers enjoy streams in wooded areas.

＊

What if there are no streams with pools of standing water near your house? Don't worry, because rain barrels are also a very good place to observe animals. Maybe you or one of your friends has one in the backyard. For some insects these are just like small pools. Mosquitoes like to lay their eggs here. The mosquito larvae eat algae growing in the barrel. As they eat, the larvae grow so much that they have to shed their skin four times.

To change from larvae to adults, the mosquitoes pupate (like caterpillars do before they turn into butterflies). The mosquito pupae hang upside down in the water with two little snorkels called trumpets sticking out from the back of their necks so they can reach the surface to breathe. If you disturb them, they'll quickly dive down and twitch madly back and forth.

＊

Now I'll tell you about animals that are very easy to observe: waterfowl. Some, like mallards, mostly swim on top of the water. Others, like mergansers, can also dive under. These birds hunt fish underwater and they can hold their breath for a very long time. It's fun to see where they pop up again. It's not always easy to guess, because you don't know which direction they're swimming when they're under the water.

IF YOU WANT TO look into a creek, take along a glass with a flat bottom. Push it into the water just far enough that water doesn't run over the lip. Now you can look into the glass and see through the bottom and sides. It's almost as good as a diving mask.

QUIZ

Why do swans have such long necks?

＊ So they can see their enemies better

＊ So they can eat underwater

With its long neck, a swan can eat plants growing underwater without having to dive to the bottom.

Barn swallows feed
their babies insects.

CHAPTER 2

WHAT ANIMALS EAT

ANIMALS HAVE THEIR FAVORITE foods, and their tastes can be quite different. Whether they like grass, fruits, insects, or even what other animals leave behind, each one will find something delicious! And animal children often need to be fed first.

DO BABY ANIMALS DRINK MILK?

Human babies drink milk, which they get from their mothers or from a bottle. It contains everything a baby needs. Some animals also get milk from their mothers, but this is not the only way.

In springtime, most animals have a rich buffet of food. Beetles like the beech-leaf miner nibble on fresh leaves.

BIG FOREST ANIMALS SUCH as wolves, foxes, and deer feed their babies milk. So do all mammals, from the tiny little shrew to the biggest whales. Whale babies drink milk from their mothers under the water. Because whales don't have lips, the babies can't suck, so mother whales squirt milk into their babies' mouths.

*

Animals that are not mammals feed their babies differently. For example, bird mothers and fathers fly home with the food their chicks need. For birds of prey this might be dead mice. They're pretty big for the beak of a little chick, so the parents rip off small pieces and hold

them out to the little ones. Chickadees and other small birds collect caterpillars that their chicks can swallow whole. So chicks eat the same food as their parents right from the beginning, which makes them different from us and other mammals.

*

Often baby animals need very different food than their parents. For example, adult frogs like to eat small aquatic animals such as crustaceans or fly larvae. They also catch insects flying by or those that have fallen into the water. Their tadpole babies, however, prefer to eat algae. This wouldn't be much good for adult frogs, but tadpoles love this green diet.

*

The larvae of many beetles are called grubs. They look like short, fat worms and some of them live underground, where they nibble on the roots of trees and bushes. The June bug is one such beetle. Over several years, its grubs feast on roots. Then one spring they'll hatch as beetles and come to the surface. There are no roots to eat anymore, so the beetles eat the fresh leaves that sprout in late spring and early summer. They are active mainly at night.

Fox kits drink milk for the
first eight weeks of their lives.

*

Bees feed their children in a different way. At first, the regular larvae get a special mixture that the bees produce called royal jelly. After a few days the nurse bees in charge of looking after the offspring change the diet. Now the bee children are fed a kind of mush made of pollen and sweet nectar. Only a few larvae continue to receive royal jelly. And it is truly royal, because these larvae will eventually become queens. (There are no kings when it comes to bees.)

*

Researchers have recently discovered a small animal that is almost like a mammal when it comes to child care. Spiders actually lay eggs like insects, and most species do not look after their offspring. The little spiders just take care of themselves after hatching. But there is a jumping spider that does the same thing as deer, pigs, or humans—she suckles her offspring. In order to do this, she produces milk on her underside for the baby spiders to drink. The spider mother feeds her children this way until they have grown enough to look after themselves.

Look!

Pygmy Shrew

THE PYGMY SHREW, OR shrewmouse as it is sometimes called, is the smallest mammal in the world. It weighs about as much as a dime (or, if you live in the UK, half as much as a 5p coin)! Shrews are actually related to hedgehogs and moles, not to mice at all. They love to eat insects, and when they're hunting, their hearts beat up to a thousand times a minute. That's ten times faster than your heart.

QUIZ

How often does
a rabbit nurse
her babies?

* Every five minutes
* Every hour
* Twice a day

The mother rabbit usually only comes to nurse her babies twice a day. It's quite normal for little rabbits to be alone most of the time. So you should never take a little rabbit that looks as if it has been abandoned. Its mother is probably on her way to feed it.

CAN ANIMALS SURVIVE ON PLANTS ALONE?

Many animals just eat plants. This makes sense, because plants can't run away. But leaves and grasses don't fill you up very quickly.

These deer are eating grass quickly, without chewing it properly.

YOU PROBABLY ALREADY KNOW that. Green salad alone isn't enough food for you. So then why don't cows or deer go hungry when they eat nothing but plants? It's simple. They eat a lot of plants. This takes many hours, because a deer needs to eat up to forty-five pounds (20 kg) of grass every day. That's about the weight of a large, fully packed suitcase!

A deer gobbles down grass because it doesn't want to spend a long time in the meadow where it can be easily spotted by predators. It would rather lie down with a full stomach in the cover of the bush or dense forest. Because it ate in a hurry and didn't chew its food well, the deer throws up small amounts of grass and then chews it again properly. That may not sound too appetizing but for the deer, it tastes as normal as it does for you to chew with your mouth full of food.

*

Eating a lot of greens can make you fart. Which is what the big herbivores do! Cows and horses have little helpers in their stomachs and intestines. These bacteria are only visible under a microscope, and yet nothing works without them. They break down the sludge of grasses and herbs even more, and only then do the animals really feel full. The bacteria create a lot of gas as they do their work. That's why herbivores not only fart, but they burp a lot, too.

*

Plants don't consist of just leaves and stems. They also have blossoms, and their flowers contain nectar that bees and butterflies drink. You may already know that. But there are many other animals that also love sweet

Flowers are like a restaurant sign to bees, "Come and enjoy some delicious nectar!"

Insect Nursery

Long-horned beetles make oval holes, because their bodies are oval.

juice, such as beetles, ants, and a kind of woodpecker called a sapsucker.

A sapsucker is far too heavy to land on a flower. It prefers to get its sweet treats from trees. It drills holes in the bark that look like many small dots close together. In the spring, tree sap flows from the bark, and the woodpecker can lick it up.

*

Many insects love dead wood. That's where they lay their eggs, and the larvae can sometimes spend years eating their way through the trunk. They live jammed in the trunk, eating the dead wood in front of them and leaving their droppings behind them. The droppings look like pressed wood powder, and they are very dry. There is no water flowing in a dead trunk, so the larvae do not pee so as not to lose too much fluid.

*

Leaves, nectar, wood. What are we missing? Fruit! Fruits and berries are important because they ripen mainly in late summer and fall. This is the time when many animals in the Northern Hemisphere are getting ready for winter. Getting ready means eating as much as possible. This makes the animals fatten up, and that's important. Later, this layer of fat under the skin will help keep them from starving when there is little food to eat over winter. Bears, which eat about twenty thousand calories a day to prepare for their winter sleep, gorge themselves on wild huckleberries and blueberries. Migratory birds search the countryside for wild cherries to give them energy for their flight south. Birds that are sticking around appreciate berries that hang on through the winter, such as the bright red berries of mountain ash.

IF YOU SEE A dead tree trunk lying on the ground, you can tell which larvae have been living there. Look at the small holes in the wood. Beetle larvae develop into adults and the adult beetles drill holes so they can get out. Beetle larvae are not the only larvae that turn into adults in the wood. If the hole is round and big enough to fit a cotton swab, it was made by a wood wasp. The hole is round because the wasp's body is round. A smaller hole would mean it was made by another insect.

QUIZ

How many ounces of eucalyptus leaves does a koala eat in one day?

* Two ounces (56 g)
* Fourteen ounces (400 g)
* Thirty-two ounces (1 kg)

Fourteen ounces (400 g). That might not sound like much but it would be like a ten-year-old child eating three pounds (1.3 kg) of salad.

WHAT HAPPENS TO ALL THE STINKY STUFF?

Every animal has to go to the bathroom. Bears, wombats, porcupines all have to do their business, several times a day, in fact.

SO WHERE IS ALL the stuff they leave behind? Shouldn't the forest floor be covered with it? But that's not the way it works.

If you go for a walk in the woods, you won't see much lying around. One of nature's little helpers is the dung beetle. They love the droppings from herbivores, especially when they are moist. They quickly dry out in the sunshine, however. So the beetles bury whatever they can, up to twenty inches (50 cm) deep. The feces will stay moist for a long time down there. This is also where the beetles lay their eggs. When the dung beetle larvae hatch, they are tucked underground, safe from birds and with their favorite food right there in front of them.

This striking-looking insect is a burying beetle.

Burying the dung is only possible if the droppings are firm. But sometimes poop comes out of big animals all runny. This happens for two reasons; if an animal is sick, it gets diarrhea, or the food is so juicy that the droppings become very wet and just splash out. This happens especially with deer in the spring, when it rains a lot. The fresh green grass contains a lot of water and very little fiber. That can make for a grumbly tummy.

But normally, poop is solid. Depending on the species, droppings will have a particular shape. Deer and hares eat nothing but plants. They produce little black-brown pellets just like sheep. Carnivores such as foxes and wolves make sausage-shaped poop that can be small or large, depending on the size of the animal. If you look closely, you can still see the fur of the animals they have eaten!

There is another food that doesn't sound very appetizing to us humans—decomposing dead animals. When a mouse dies, it will eventually start to stink and the smell attracts a special kind of beetle. The burying beetle has pretty orange and black stripes. It will smell the dead mouse right away. The beetle doesn't come alone, but as a couple, a female and male. The two immediately begin to bury the dead mouse so no flies will lay eggs on it and no fox will grab it. Under the ground, the beetle couple kneads the mouse into a kind of meatball. They also wet the body with a liquid to keep the meat fresh longer. Finally, the female lays eggs. Once the larvae hatch, the parents feed them the meat of the dead mouse.

Individual dung balls indicate that the food was quite dry.

Look!

Vitamin Balls

RABBITS AND GUINEA PIGS have a special relationship with their poop. They love to eat grass and leaves, but sometimes they also nibble on their own droppings. That sounds disgusting, but for rodents it's as important as it is for you to eat fruit. Their poop actually contains many vitamins. If the animals don't eat the pellets, they'll become ill.

QUIZ

How long is the world's longest tapeworm?

* Three feet (1 m)
* Thirty-two feet (10 m)
* Sixty-five feet (20 m)

About sixty-five feet (20 m). The fish tapeworm develops inside fish. If dogs, cats, or even humans eat the fish raw, the tapeworm can continue to grow to its full length inside them. (Fortunately, this happens very rarely.)

HOW DO ANIMALS AVOID BECOMING DINNER?

You probably already know that big animals eat smaller ones. But who wants to end up inside another animal's stomach? Smaller animals have come up with many different ways to make sure this doesn't happen—to too many of them, at least.

This moth has double protection. It is the same color as dry grass, where it sleeps all day long. And it has fluffy scales, which absorb the cries of bats.

THE BEST STRATEGY IS not to be seen in the first place so you might try to hide. And if you don't want to do that, you could disguise yourself. In Australia, there is a spider that looks and smells like bird droppings. It even spins whitish silk that looks like spattered poop. What bird would want to eat that? Then there are animals that blend in with their surroundings using camouflage. That's why pond frogs are green. You can only tell them apart from the water plants if they are moving.

Birds like to eat moths. So many moths fly around at night, when they are hard to see. But moths can also be found through sound.

Bats have always had an appetite for moths. To catch them, the bats call loudly and often. We can't hear these calls because they are very high-pitched. The bats are actually listening for a tiny little echo. An echo that may have bounced off the body of a moth.

Mind you, the moths have a good defense. Their dense, furry coats absorb the bats' cries instead of echoing them back, so the bats can't find the moths as easily.

By the way, moths also have excellent hearing. Even though they have very small ears, they recognize the high-pitched cries of bats. When they realize that a bat is nearby, they may simply just let themselves fall into the grass, where the bat won't find them.

Animals that don't hide or use camouflage may defend themselves in other ways. A hedgehog, for instance, has many sharp quills. It just curls up into a spiny ball

Orange and black stripes
signal "Danger!"

Puffer Fish

SOMETIMES ANIMALS WANT TO say to other animals, "I'm big so you can't eat me!" Fish often down their meals in one gulp, so puffer fish that think they might be on the menu swallow water, which makes them inflate like balloons so they are bigger than a bite-sized meal. Some puff up to the size of a beach ball. Puffer fish live mostly in warm ocean waters. The black-saddled puffer fish, for instance, lives on the Great Barrier Reef in Australia.

when it is attacked. Our dog once tried to bite a hedgehog. It hurt his mouth so much that he never tried to do it again!

*

Some insects defend themselves with poison. The caterpillar of the cinnabar moth eats poisonous ragwort, which can be dangerous even to humans. (Imagine if we confused it with salad greens and ate large amounts by mistake.) The caterpillars aren't harmed by the poison, but they then become poisonous themselves. If a bird tries to eat one, it can die. So the birds leave these caterpillars alone.

But how do they know which ones to avoid? This particular caterpillar has black and orange stripes. This is not a disguise, it's actually a warning. All animals know that species with these striking colors can be dangerous.

Do you know other flashy-looking animals? Perhaps you've already met a wasp. Wasps can sting, and they warn others away with their black-and-yellow coats. The fire salamander also wears yellow and black as a warning. It has glands that contain a poisonous liquid. And nobody wants to eat that.

*

But what if all these strategies don't work? Well, you can still run away, if you're quick. Rabbits and hares are very fast runners. First they will crouch down in the grass and try to hide. But if a fox gets too close, they dash away like the wind, back and forth in a zigzag pattern. No fox or dog can run that fast, or change direction so quickly.

QUIZ

If you hear barking in the forest, is it most likely coming from

* A deer
* A fox
* A wolf

A deer. When deer are frightened, they make a barking sound to warn other deer.

A clump of frog's eggs is called frog spawn.

CHAPTER 3

ALL ABOUT ANIMAL BABIES

MANY BABY ANIMALS HATCH FROM eggs. Insects, frogs, and birds all develop inside fluid-filled pouches that may or may not be protected by a shell. It's easier for a mother to lay eggs than carry live babies in her belly, so these animal children tend to have many siblings. Mammals carry live babies. They usually have fewer of them, but they take care of them for a longer time.

WHO LIKES IT COOL AND WET?

Frogs and toads lay eggs. Their eggs are as soft as jelly and they dry out quickly, so the parents mate in the water.

The male midwife toad carries the eggs on his body until the tadpoles hatch.

THE EGGS ARE LAID while the parents are still mating. Apparently amphibians like to do things in a hurry!

It's easy to tell the difference between frog eggs and toad eggs. With the common frog, the eggs hang together in large clusters. Toad eggs are joined together in long strings. You can find the eggs in March in shallow water along the shores of ponds, where it's easier for the sun to keep them warm.

*

Because the eggs are transparent, you can see how much the tadpoles inside have developed. At the beginning they look like little black dots. But after just a few days they have stretched out and are shaped like a small fish. At some point the egg becomes too small for them, and they force their way out through the slimy outside layer.

Midwife toads do it differently. To make sure no other animals eat the eggs, the father wraps the egg strands around his hind legs.

The parents and offspring may meet up again someday, since frogs and toads always return to the pond where they hatched. Do the children and parents recognize each other? Unfortunately, researchers have not yet studied this, so I couldn't tell you.

Salamander larvae do not breathe through their mouths but through gills at the back of their heads.

*

The fire salamander lives in Europe. It is related to frogs, yet it also does many things differently. The salamander children develop inside the mother's belly, just like human babies. The pregnancy also lasts for up to nine months, which is similar to humans. Like frogs, however, salamanders give birth in the water. The salamander mother looks for a forest stream where there are no fish, since she doesn't want her children to be eaten. Over several days, she gives birth to up to thirty of them! The little ones are not yet black and yellow like their parents. But they can take care of themselves right away, catching small crustaceans to eat.

*

Lizards are not amphibians like frogs, toads, and newts, although they look a bit like salamanders. Because they are reptiles, they live on land and all but a few lay eggs. They look like little bird's eggs and have a white shell. But unlike birds, lizards cannot hatch their eggs by sitting on them. Their bodies are just too cold for that. They only warm up when everything around them is warm. So the lizard mothers prefer to bury their eggs in a sunny spot. The ground is warm enough that the lizard babies hatch after about two months.

*

The common European lizard stores her eggs in her body to keep them nice and warm until just before her babies hatch. At birth the babies are still wrapped in a soft membrane that they quickly break out of. Lizard children have to be careful, because shortly after birth their own mother does not recognize them anymore. Instead, she may think the tiny creature in front of her is her dinner!

TRY THIS!

LIZARDS LIKE TO LIVE in gardens. They need small piles of wood or stones to hide in, otherwise they may be eaten by cats. These piles are not difficult to build, you just heap everything together. Once the pile is finished, you shouldn't change it. You never know whether a lizard or other animal is already living inside.

QUIZ

How big is the world's largest salamander?

* Eight inches (20 cm)
* Twenty inches (50 cm)
* Sixty inches (150 cm)

The biggest salamander is the Japanese giant salamander. It grows up to sixty inches (150 cm) long and weighs up to sixty-five pounds (30 kg).

HOW DO INSECTS LOOK AFTER THEIR BABIES?

Insect babies are sometimes born without their parents around. But they're not completely on their own when they hatch. Most of the time they are with their many siblings, and their parents have ingenious ways of helping them survive even if they are not around.

Butterflies need meadows with wildflowers.

BY THE TIME CATERPILLARS emerge from their cocoons, their parents are long gone. But that doesn't mean they haven't taken care of the little ones. Mother swallowtail butterflies, for instance, carefully decide exactly where to lay their eggs. The caterpillars need to have enough to eat as soon as they hatch. And no one will be around to show them which plants are poisonous and which are not. So the butterfly mothers check out everything ahead of time. They stomp around on a leaf and can sense through their feet whether they're on the right plant species. Only then do they lay their eggs. And when the tiny caterpillars hatch, they're sitting right on one of their favorite foods, such as Queen Anne's lace.

*

Gall midges and gall wasps lay their eggs on leaves. Before long, the leaves form a small ball (gall) around the egg. These galls can be pointy or round like a tiny ball of wool. Inside each one there's a larva that can develop well protected from birds. So each gall basically contains an only child. The larva keeps eating bits from the inside of the ball and grows until it pupates. When the transformation is complete and the new wasp wants to hatch, it eats a small hole in the wall. You can tell whether anything is still living in a gall—if there is no hole, the gall is still occupied.

*

A tiny larva lives inside this big round gall.

Parasitic wasps have a completely different way of raising their young. They lay their eggs inside the larvae of other insects. The tiny wasp children are well protected in there! They now eat their host slowly from the inside out. Doesn't sound too nice, does it? And it's still very dangerous. If a bird eats the host, it swallows the small parasitic wasps inside it as well.

*

Other insects look after their offspring with great care. Bees feed their larvae, defend them against enemies, and keep them warm. The larvae grow up in a kind of kinder-garten. While their mother, the queen, lays eggs and has little time or energy left over for them, the worker bees take care of the offspring until they are adults.

*

Although spiders are not insects, they look similar. They lay eggs, too, but they don't just leave them lying on leaves. Instead, the spiders pack the eggs inside cocoons, so they won't be easily gobbled up by other small animals. The cocoons are little balls of spider silk that look like cotton wool. Some spiders hide these cocoons—perhaps tucked under tree bark. Others carry them around on their abdomen. After the little ones hatch, some mothers drag them around on their back. With over one hundred babies, that can be pretty exhausting!

Look!

Counting Legs

Wolf spiders are very common. With a bit of patience, you might be able to spot a mother carrying her babies on her back.

IT'S EASY TO TELL the difference between spiders and insects. Insects have antennae, six legs, and usually have wings. Spiders, on the other hand, have eight legs, no antennae, and no wings. In most insects, the body is divided into three parts: head, thorax, and abdomen. The spider's body consists of only two parts.

TRY THIS!

THE ONLY PLANT THE striped caterpillars of the monarch butterfly eat is milkweed. If you live in North America, you can help monarchs by planting milkweed. But make sure you plant it somewhere your pets can't get to it, because it is poisonous to humans and pets. Its milky sap will also irritate your skin and be really painful if it gets in your eyes, so be careful if you get near it.

WHY DO BIRDS LAY EGGS?

Birds lay eggs, and these eggs are quite big in relation to the size of the mother bird's body. So why don't the little ones grow up inside the mother's belly to be born as chicks?

MOST BIRDS RAISE FOUR or five children at a time. If they were all born at the same time, like mammal babies, they wouldn't all fit inside their mother's belly and with all those big eggs inside her, the mother bird would be too heavy to take off. That's why the eggs are laid at intervals over several days, so there is plenty of space in her belly for each one.

Some bird parents start to brood or sit on the eggs after the last egg has been laid. Only then do the chicks begin to develop inside the shell. And because all the eggs are incubated at the same time, it doesn't take long for all the siblings to hatch as big strong chicks who will grow up quickly. During brooding, the eggs must stay warm. There's no heater in the nest, so for most birds either the parents take turns sitting on the eggs and keeping them warm with their bodies or one parent does nothing but sit on the eggs while the other goes out to find food. To make sure the chicks don't stick to the inside of the shell, the parents turn the eggs over at regular intervals. Brooding for most, but not all, species takes two to four weeks. Male emperor penguins, for instance, are super dads in the bird world. They balance a single egg on their feet, tucked up under their feathers, for up to seventy-five days. They eat a lot beforehand so they don't have to eat while they are keeping their egg warm.

*

Just before the chicks hatch, they begin to peep inside their shells. They're calling their parents, who answer back. This way, everyone gets to know each other even before birth, which means that later, the chicks and parents recognize each other mainly by voice. This is especially important for birds that breed in large communities. Penguins, for instance, live in huge colonies, with hundreds of thousands of chicks. When the parents come ashore from the sea and want to go to their chicks, things can become quite confused. Parents and penguin children only find each other again by recognizing their unique calls.

Emus lay between five and fifteen eggs at a time and may lay up to fifty eggs a year. The eggs are five inches (12 cm) long and weigh one to two pounds (0.5 to 1 kg).

Hatching out of the egg is exhausting work. The chicks have to peck away at the eggshell and make a hole that they can crawl out of. They have a special small tooth for this on their beaks. It is very hard and helps break up the shell. This tooth falls off a short time later.

By the time the chicks finally make it out of the shell, they are very tired. They also get cold quickly because they are still naked and wet, so the parents keep them warm for a while. In some species, such as ducks, owls, and domestic chickens, the chicks have very small feathers right from the start. These feathers, which begin to grow fast, are very fluffy and look more like fur. The chicks can't fly with these feathers, but that would be too dangerous anyway. They are blind in the first days, because their eyes are still closed.

The chicks grow quickly and soon get their adult feathers. Most songbird children can fly after three weeks. They'll leave the nest but stay close by for a few days. During this time, the parents still feed them occasionally. They're not that afraid of people yet, so if you're careful, you can sometimes get close enough to watch them. But don't try to catch them or move them, or their parents won't be able to find them again.

I'm first! As long as the other chicks are still in their shells, the first hatchling gets all the caterpillars that the parents bring to the nest.

TRY THIS!

BIRD PARENTS THROW THE eggshells out of the nest to make more room for the chicks. You can collect these empty shells and check the internet to see which species they come from. Then you'll know what kind of chicks are growing up nearby. Robins have particularly beautiful blue eggs.

QUIZ

Which bird has the most chicks?

* Partridge
* Robin
* Golden eagle

It's the partridge, which lays up to twenty eggs. Partridges spend most of their time on the ground, which is a dangerous place for a bird, so they need to lay lots of eggs to make sure at least some of their babies survive.

ARE BABIES BETTER THAN EGGS?

The name "mammal" comes from the Latin word for breast, since all mammal babies, from humans and monkeys to whales, drink milk from their mothers.

A foal can stand up just fifteen minutes after being born, and it can walk soon after.

MAMMAL BABIES DEVELOP INSIDE their mothers' bellies. This takes much longer than in animals like birds and insects, whose young develop inside eggs. That's why mammals usually mate in the fall or winter. After a few months, the babies are born in the spring, when nature provides lots to eat. The mothers need to eat well so they can produce enough milk.

*

Grizzly bears, however, mate in the spring, so the cubs would normally be born in the fall, but then they would still be very small when winter hits. So grizzly bears do something special. The baby doesn't begin to grow in the mother's belly until late fall and is born in mid-winter, when the mother is still in her cozy den. By the time the cub is large enough to leave, the weather is nice and warm, and the meadows are full of juicy greens.

*

But why don't mammals, including humans, just lay eggs? Because most mammal babies take a long time to develop, eggs lying in a nest would be at risk for too

Look!

Platypus

THERE IS A MAMMAL in Australia that does things very differently. The platypus lays her eggs in a burrow she digs in a riverbank. When the young hatch, the mother "sweats" milk from her skin for her babies to drink.

long. The eggs of insects and birds can be discovered and eaten by other animals, such as martens. Mammal babies are much better protected inside the mother's belly.

*

But babies in the belly are also at a disadvantage. A mother wild boar, for example, can no longer run as quickly when she's pregnant, so she can be caught more easily by predators. And giving birth is an especially dangerous time, because the mother can't run away. A female wild boar hides in the bushes, so that wolves or bears can't see her.

*

After the babies are born, they can start to drink their mother's milk. During the first few days they may be blind and helpless and have to sleep a lot. They also can't run fast, so they often stay home while their parents go out to look for food. With wolves, aunts or uncles watch over the little ones. Deer often leave their babies on their own. But the young are almost odorless and hard to see in the grass or bush because of the spots on their fur.

*

With animals that live in wide grasslands like horses, newborns can often run after just a few hours. This is important because horses or wild cattle live in large herds, and they won't wait long for stragglers. It's much safer in a herd, where the youngsters run between adults who protect them from predators. That's why mothers hurry back to the herd with their offspring as soon as possible after giving birth.

Most mammals have nipples so they can nurse their young or udders between their back legs, like cows and horses.

A mother opossum carries her babies on her back.

CHAPTER 4

HOW ANIMALS GROW UP

NOT ALL ANIMALS LIVE IN FAMILIES. Insect children are happy growing up in kindergartens without adults. Seals are sociable, but they like to keep their distance, too. Wolves do things the way we do. They like to stick together, snuggle up close, and help each other throughout their lives.

HOW IMPORTANT ARE FAMILIES?

Many fish are very sociable. Yet most species do not live in families. The mother fish lays her eggs in a small hollow in the bottom of a stream and then swims away. Like fish, many insects can be found in large groups, but not always for the same reasons.

On a sunny summer day you may be able to see fish kindergartens.

IN SOME SPECIES LIKE salmon, the parents die right after the eggs are laid, so the fish are already orphans by the time they hatch. Fish children live dangerous lives, because bigger fish are always hungry and they hunt the small ones. That's why fish children prefer to form small schools and swim in the shallow water near the shore, where the bigger fish can't follow them.

*

Fish children aren't lonely. Since they have no parents, they watch out for each other. When many young fish swim together in a school, it's harder for a big fish to catch a small one. Which one should it take? This one? Or that one over there? The school is constantly moving this way and that. The fish bodies glisten in the sunlight and confuse the attacker. So it will catch only the occasional small fish, and many of the others will live to grow up. Even as adults, fish often stay together in a school. The herring that live in the sea form huge schools, where all the fish swim together in the same direction. So instead of having families, some fish have many friends that they spend all their time with.

Mosquitoes and fish have a lot in common. Female mosquitoes lay their eggs in water, usually in small pools. When the larvae hatch, they'll often stay together in kindergartens. If a newt or fish comes to eat them, they'll jerk like crazy all together in the water, which totally confuses the hunter.

Adult mosquitoes fly together in swarms, just like many fish swim together in schools. But they don't do this to defend themselves against enemies. In many species, the swarms consist only of males. They float up and down like a cloud, giving off an enticing smell. The females are drawn to it and fly into the cloud to mate with the fragrant males. (By the way, you don't have to be afraid of these mosquito clouds. Male mosquitoes don't sting—only the females do.)

Unlike mosquitoes or fish, beetles are usually loners. The larvae of ladybird beetles live on leaves, where they hunt aphids. Even when they become adults, they prefer to be alone. But in fall, ladybird beetles often find themselves together in large clusters. These are not true swarms, because the ladybird beetles don't fly around together. They are just looking for a winter home, where they can spend the cold season together. This could be a crevice in a house or in an attic crawl space, if they can find a way to get in. Ladybird beetles cuddle up because they like to wake up together after hibernation. The males and females mate in the spring, and that way they don't have to spend a long time searching for a partner.

Look!

Stick Insects

STICK INSECTS GET THEIR name because they are long and thin—and look like sticks. Female stick insects don't need to find a mate every time they want to have babies. They just lay eggs and walk away. All the babies that hatch will be clones (exact copies) of their mother. Once in a while, she has to find a mate to make sure not every stick insect out there is a clone. You can find stick insects in many backyards in Australia. They like peace and quiet and lots of eucalyptus leaves to eat.

QUIZ

About how many aphids will a ladybird larva eat before it pupates and becomes a beetle?

* Fifty
* Five hundred
* Five thousand

A larva will eat (or lick up, more accurately speaking) about five hundred aphids.

DO BABY ANIMALS HAVE To FEND FOR THEMSELVES?

Many birds and mammals only look after their children for one summer, or, at most, for the first year of life. After that, the families break up.

The patches on this fawn's coat look like the sun's rays falling on the grass.

THIS IS WHAT HAPPENS with deer, for example. The fawns are often left on their own in the grass during the first weeks, while the mother searches for food. Only after a few weeks will they always be found at their mother's side, because by then they can run almost as fast as she can. The following spring, when new fawns are born, the older siblings from the previous year have to leave. That's not a bad thing, because they are now adults and can take care of themselves. When the time comes, the mother scares the older sibling away.

Adult deer live alone from spring to fall. If another deer comes along, it is chased away.

*

In winter, the deer join together to form groups. The animals are not necessarily related or even friends. But they don't want to fight over territory, because fighting consumes a lot of energy. The deer would be hungrier and in winter there is not much to eat. That's why they get along with each other and often stand together. Even if they are not really friends, there are still big advantages to staying in a group like this. If a predator approaches, the deer will notice it faster than if they are on their own.

*

Seals do much the same thing. They, too, prefer to live in a group, but not all snuggled up together. Seal children just stay with their mothers for about five weeks. They only feel truly safe in the water because they move

Sea Otters

Who's been nibbling on these cones?

QUIZ

* A woodpecker
* A mouse
* A squirrel

A squirrel—it rips off the scales. Mice will nibble a cone neatly and smoothly, and wood-peckers chop up the cone until it's in pieces.

THE SEA OTTER IS the largest member of the weasel family. It spends almost all its life in the ocean. Mother sea otters carry their babies on their chests and spend a lot of time grooming them to keep their fur fluffy and waterproof. Females like to raft up together and when they are resting, they wrap themselves in fronds of kelp (a kind of seaweed that is anchored to the ocean floor) to keep them from drifting apart.

very slowly on land, so they'll lie right at the edge of the shore, where they can quickly slip back into the water. Seals lying together on a sandbank are careful to keep their distance from one another. They don't like each other that much, but they don't like to be alone, either.

*

Raven parents stay together their whole lives. But their children leave the family when they grow up. The young ravens form great swarms and move out into the world. So they stay together, but with friends, not family.

*

Although squirrels like to cozy up together, most of them prefer to live on their own, except for mothers that have just had children. The little ones stay with her for almost a year, even if they are able to look after themselves before this. When they are adults, they part ways. There are no permanent squirrel families. In spite of this, sometimes a few squirrels get together to share the same nest, or drey. So they are not true loners.

DO ANIMAL FAMILIES STAY TOGETHER FOREVER?

Wolves and field mice live in close family groups. Foxes roam far from their families. Every family is different.

Granny, one of the most famous orcas in the Pacific Northwest, swims with the big male Ruffles, named because of the curves in his huge dorsal fin.

WOLVES LIKE TO BE close together, so the whole big family lives in one place. The pack shares the work and hunts together. Even the old wolves stay in the pack and are looked after. Wolves also have a kindergarten. When the parents go out to hunt for food, the offspring stay at home near the den, and other relatives take care of the little ones.

There are special groups of killer whales, or orcas, on the Northwest Coast of North America. They are known as residents, and each family group, or pod, is led by an experienced older female, who decides where the family should travel to find the salmon they feed on. (Although other orcas in these waters and around the world feed on marine mammals, the resident whales eat only salmon.) The females share the fish they catch, and their children stay with them all their lives. Males are larger and not as good at catching fish. If a male's mother dies and food is scarce, he may have difficulty catching fish to feed himself. We know so much about these orcas because each whale can be identified by the shape of its big dorsal fin that sticks up out of the water and the patterns of the saddle patch below the fin.

From dolphins to cows, most mammals prefer to stay together as a family. Even field mice are very sociable. They like to live in families or in large groups. The females will even take care of a stranger's baby and nurse it.

*

Sometimes it is hard to tell that foxes live with their families. This is because foxes have large territories and often travel alone. But they still stick together in large groups, much like wolves. Because we mostly see them on their own, people have long thought that foxes were loners, but it turns out that they just need a bit more space.

*

Wild boars are family oriented, but it's often just the mother and her children who really live together. As soon as the young ones grow up, the male offspring go out on their own. The female pigs often stay with the family at first, but at some point they will go out looking for their own territory.

*

So how many animals really stay as a family forever? We can't know for sure. But wild boars have a special quality that other animals, including other mammals, do not possess. If a child returns to the mother as an adult one day, the mother will recognize it as a relative. Otherwise she would fight strange boars and drive them out of her territory.

TRY THIS!

BATS LIKE TO LIVE in family colonies of hundreds or even thousands of individuals. If you would like to see bats, you don't need to stay up late at night. Little brown bats fly shortly after dusk to catch moths and mosquitoes. Because they like to roost in attics, you can often spot them in your backyard.

Look!

Beavers

BEAVERS MATE FOR LIFE and raise their young together. Their teeth are so strong that they can cut down trees with them. They do this to get at the leaves and bark at the top of the tree, which they love to eat. Then they use the branches to build large shelters in the water. To keep out other animals, they dam up streams with the branches to create large ponds. The entrances to their shelters, known as lodges, are now underwater and only the beavers can get in, because they are good divers. This is where they live with their families.

WHAT HAPPENS WHEN ANIMALS GET OLD?

Like us, animals eventually grow old. Maybe they can't run so fast anymore. They become weaker, and they start to turn gray.

Old horses need lots of love, and they can return it, too.

WE ALL NOTICE THIS when our pets get older. Horses lose their big back teeth one after the other. That makes it harder for them to chew grass. Partly chewed grass isn't as easy to digest, so the horses grow thinner. They may also become lame, because they don't move around as much and therefore have less muscle. Have you ever watched a horse stand up? It takes momentum and power, and you can only do this if you're strong. This means old horses don't like to lie down, because they don't know whether they'll be able to get up again.

*

In the wild, old horses can still help the herd. They've learned a lot during their long lives. You don't have to be the fastest to be useful to the herd. To live for a long time, you need to know when something is dangerous.

It could be a river that is too deep and flows too fast to cross, or a mountain lion that's about to attack. Young horses may have never seen a mountain lion, so they don't know to run away unless an old horse warns them. Young horses may also not know about good things. Where is the juiciest grass? Where can you find something to drink in a dry summer? Where can you go to find protection from the wind during a storm? Old animals can show the others, because they have been in these situations before.

*

Old animals can be cranky more often than young ones. They find things much more difficult because their hearing and eyesight aren't as good. They may have painful joints, which doesn't help anyone's mood. If you have an old pet, you should be patient with it. Old animals often like to sleep a little more.

*

Older dogs may not want to play as much. You know how you get out of breath more when you run around? Aging dogs may only want to play for a short time because they find it exhausting. This isn't because they don't like you as much—love is as strong in old animals as it is in young ones.

*

The coat of old horses and goats changes, too. Normally, the winter coat falls out within a few weeks after it gets warm. But generating new hair takes a lot of energy, so old animals take their time to do this, even if it means they get hotter on warm spring days and can look pretty shaggy while their old winter coats grow out.

*

Something else changes, too—the coat color. Animals turn gray, the same way older people do. But with any luck, they don't complain about it!

QUIZ

Which animal can grow especially old?

* A mouse
* A clam
* A whale

Mice don't live for more than six years. Bowhead whales can be more than two hundred years old. But a species of ocean clam found in the cold North Sea was found to be more than five hundred years old!

Baby cottontails are
safe in their burrow.

CHAPTER 5

ANIMAL SURVIVAL TECHNIQUES

ANIMALS DON'T HAVE CENTRAL heating or umbrellas, and they can't just pop out to the grocery store for food. They have clever ways of looking after themselves, but they may also need you to help keep the places they call home clean and safe.

HOW DO ANIMALS STAY WARM AND DRY?

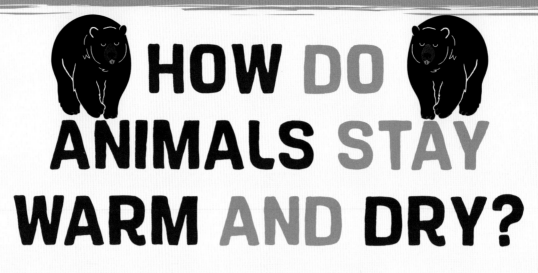

Nobody really likes rain—except maybe fish and frogs. Because for people and for animals, when you're wet, you're cold.

The swallow's feathers are tightly layered.

FORTUNATELY, MANY ANIMALS HAVE something like a raincoat. A bird's feathers are layered like roof shingles, so the rain can run down without touching their skin. Only when it rains long and hard do the drops run between the feathers. Then the birds shake themselves vigorously to get rid of the water.

*

Animals with fur can also cope with a little rain. Their fur is oily, so the drops of water bead off. The same

thing happens with your hair, too. But because humans shampoo regularly to keep their hair clean, we lose this protection. We may think this looks nicer, but it's not actually practical in the rain. Luckily we have umbrellas and raincoats!

Animals don't know about shampoo, so their fur protects them if the rain is light. During big downpours, deer seek shelter under trees, where it is drier. As soon as the sun shines again, they'll run to the nearest clearing to let their coats dry.

The shaggy winter coats of bison insulate them so well that when snow lands on their backs it doesn't even melt.

There is one animal that really doesn't get along with rain at all. Earthworms live in tunnels that they dig up to ten feet (3 m) deep into the ground. To keep these tunnels open they coat the inside with slime. Usually there's still enough air to breathe down there but when it rains, you see earthworms everywhere, because they crawl out of the ground. They don't do this because they like to get wet. On the contrary, they are in danger of drowning! When it rains a lot all at once, the holes in the ground fill up with water, including the tunnels belonging to the earthworms. The worms have to get up to the air fast.

And how do they know that the weather is bad? It's easy. They can hear and feel the first pitter-patter of drops on the ground. That gives them enough time to crawl up and out.

*

When it's cold out, people just dress in warmer clothes. And because it's not so pleasant outside, we'll spend more time indoors in winter. Some animals need a warm layer in the winter, too. Of course, they can't just pull on a change of clothes. But many species protect their bodies with fur or feathers. Their coats are not so thick in the summer, so that more air can reach the skin. This allows the animals to cool off more easily when it's hot. In the fall, when it gets cooler, a new layer of fur or feathers grows in. It is much thicker and fluffier and holds the heat well.

IF YOU WANT TO see earthworms, you can try luring them out of the ground. Take two sticks and bang them on the lawn or flower bed for about ten minutes. After a while the worms will come up to see if it's raining. The drumming sounds like water drops. When they realize the weather is nice, they'll disappear back into their holes.

HOW DO ANIMALS COOL DOWN?

Most animals enjoy warm weather. Only animals like polar bears favor the cold. But when the temperature rises to more than eighty-five degrees Fahrenheit (30°C), that's too hot for most species.

When kangaroos get too hot, they give themselves a saliva bath. They lick the fur on their forearms until it is all wet, then they cool down as their fur dries out.

IT'S NOT SO BAD for humans, we can just sweat and this keeps our skin moist and cool. But many animals, such as crows, cannot sweat. Not only that, but crow feathers are black, and they heat up faster in the sun than light-colored birds like gulls. So they have just two choices. Either the crow flies into the shade, or it opens its beak wide and caws. Because the inside of its body is even warmer than the outside air, the air cools the bird when the crow quickly inhales and exhales. Dogs do exactly the same thing—they breathe hard and let their tongues hang out. Their tongue is wet and quickly cools as the dogs pant.

*

Hot sunshine can be dangerous for animals that have moist bodies. They can't let themselves dry out, otherwise they'll die. Salamanders, who prefer to move at night and in the rain, bury themselves in damp soil during the day. A rotten log is also a good hiding place because it stores water like a sponge. It's nice and cool underneath, even on dry summer days.

*

Snails aren't great diggers, especially since they carry their house around with them. To make sure they don't dry out, they'll retreat right into their house and close the entrance with a layer of mucus. (When it dries, it looks like a sheet of plastic wrap.)

*

Bees have a different problem. Inside a beehive, the honeycombs are made of wax, and they can melt if it gets too warm. To prevent this, many bees are sent to the hive entrance. You can sometimes hear the thrumming sound as they flap their wings to fan cool air into the hive. The bees also distribute water on the honey-combs. The draft of air wafts through the hive and cools it down.

*

There are a few animal species that sweat. Horses, for example, get soaking wet when they get too warm. But any creature that sweats also gets very thirsty, so horses need a lot of water when it's hot—just like humans.

*

Pigs have found another way to cool off. They wallow in a pool of mud. This can be a small pond or forest spring—the main thing is that there is a lot of mud. The pigs lie down in it and roll around so that as much mud as possible sticks to their body. This cools them off nicely, and when they get warm again, they just go back to the mudhole for another round.

*

The only creatures that can't sweat and bathe are animals that live in the water. It's already wet there, so sweating wouldn't do much good. Fish just dive a little deeper when it gets hot, because the water is cooler deeper down.

TRY THIS!

JUST LIKE YOU, BIRDS get thirsty and like to cool off when the weather is warm. Why not add a birdbath to your backyard? It should be wide and not too deep, with a rough surface (birds don't like slippery pools any more than you do). Put it out in an open space so the birds can keep an eye out for danger, and make sure you change the water often.

Look!

Summer Concert

GRASSHOPPERS ARE LIKE LIVING thermometers—you just have to listen for them. If it's cooler than fifty-four degrees Fahrenheit (12°C), the grasshoppers are silent. But when it reaches this temperature, they'll begin to chirp very slowly. The higher the temperature, the faster the chirping becomes. If you practice comparing the temperature on the thermometer with the chirping speed, at some point you'll be able to hear how warm it is, even without a thermometer.

CAN THERE BE TOO MANY ANIMALS?

There are rarely too many animals. You might think that mice, for example, could multiply so much that they would soon cover every surface. So why don't they?

Mouse children are already grown up at the age of two weeks, and they can have their own babies when they are three weeks old.

ONE PAIR OF MICE CAN produce up to two thousand children, grandchildren, and great-grandchildren a year. But that doesn't actually happen, for good reason. When there are many animals, diseases spread more quickly. The mice meet other mice more often and even if only one of them has a bad illness, the others quickly get infected. There are no vaccinations for mice. Sick mice are also more likely to be caught by a fox or buzzard because they can't run away as fast, so there will be even fewer.

Deer also become stressed if there are too many of them. When this happens, they can no longer all find their own territory, and they are constantly being driven out by other deer. The animals are afraid and angry, and they produce fewer fawns. Instead of two or three, they may have just one per year. And if fewer fawns are born, the population drops again.

If there are too many animals of one kind, there is often not enough food to go around. I have seen a forest where the caterpillars ate the trees completely bare.

There were so many caterpillars that you could hear the sound of their droppings in the forest. At the end of the spring, the trees had no leaves and the caterpillars were out of food. In addition, as with the mice, diseases spread. Hungry and sick, the caterpillars could not hold out. In the end, not many survived, and the trees were able to recover.

＊

Another effect of too many caterpillars is that it causes bird numbers to grow. If they find lots of caterpillars to feed their chicks, they may breed twice or even three times in spring and summer, instead of just once. The many young birds that leave the nest are hungry and keep eating the caterpillars. This stops the caterpillars from eating the trees bare, and that's good news for the trees.

＊

Too many deer can also threaten the trees of a forest. In spring and summer there is plenty for deer to eat in the fields, where the farmers grow cereals and vegetables for us humans. And lush grass grows in the meadows, to make hay for the cows. The deer love all these plants growing in the fields and meadows. They have loads of food, so the deer calves grow up healthy.

However, in winter, the meadows and fields are harvested. The hungry deer head into the forest, where they are desperate enough to eat the small trees, making it hard for a new forest to regrow.

But if a wolf pack settles in the area, everything changes. The hungry wolves chase the deer. That way there are fewer deer, and more small trees can grow. So in this case, the wolf is a friend to the forest.

QUIZ

How many droppings does a caterpillar make in the few weeks until it pupates?

＊ About one hundred

＊ About one thousand

＊ About ten thousand

A caterpillar makes about one thousand droppings before it pupates and turns into a butterfly.

Look!

Tent Caterpillars

TENT CATERPILLARS EAT THE leaves of trees. These moth larvae build big weblike nests or "tents," where they are safe from predators. Some years you hardly notice them, and other years there are masses of them wriggling around. There can be so many that they eat the trees bare early in the season. Luckily the trees have time to grow new leaves before fall, so they rarely die unless they are already stressed.

WHAT'S IT LIKE TO LIVE WITH GARBAGE?

There is no garbage in the animal world. Anything that is no longer needed just rots and becomes earth all over again.

You can do your bit by making sure you don't leave litter lying around.

OF COURSE, ANIMALS DO leave behind a kind of waste. Leftover food, for example. When wolves eat an elk, bones remain. But then mice will come and gnaw on them. Flies also love bones, especially the marrow inside them. So after a few months the remains of a wolf's meal may disappear without a trace.

＊

Even the hair that horses, cows, and deer lose when they change their coats is not harmful. Birds use it to cushion their nests and keep them cozy and warm.

Some moths also like hair—they lay their eggs in it, and the larvae eat the hair.

＊

But human garbage doesn't do animals any good at all. Fiberglass insulation, for example, is very harmful. It is used to insulate homes so they don't need to be heated so much. But if it lies around in nature, birds build their nests with it, because they think it's hair. The glass fibers can cut the naked chicks so badly they will die.

Plastic is a much bigger problem. Left lying around, it will eventually break up into very tiny pieces. These are eaten by earthworms or sucked up by wasps when they drink water from a puddle. The plastic stays in the bodies of these animals and makes them sick. When larger animals such as birds or hedge-hogs eat these earthworms and wasps, the plastic also gets into their bodies. At some point, all animals have small bits of plastic in them. That's why it's so important to throw plastic garbage in the trash and never leave any plastic outside. It would be even better if we stopped using plastic bottles, plastic bags, and other things made of plastic.

Sometimes bottles and cans can be dangerous for individual animals. A fox or a skunk may stick their heads inside one, wondering what smells so delicious in there. Then the animal can't pull its head out again and it might run around for a while with the can on its head. Hopefully it will find someone to help. Otherwise it won't be able to drink or eat anything ever again.

Animals can die not just from garbage, but also from poison. These poisons, known as pesticides, are sprayed on farm crops such as corn or on trees like pines to protect them from caterpillars. But the pesticide kills not just the caterpillars, but all insects. And not just insects. Birds that feed on caterpillars starve to death when there are none left. That's why it's good to see more and more people farming their land without using pesticides. They can only do that if people are willing to spend a bit more money on organic food in the supermarket. Farmers who grow food without using pesticides leave part of the fruit behind for animals like caterpillars. Because the animals don't pay money for this fruit, people have to be willing to make up the difference.

Fences can be dangerous, too. Often they are still covered with barbed wire, which can really hurt if you run into it by mistake. The wire consists of many metal spikes, which can cut deep into the flesh. So it's good to stop using barbed wire and to completely take down these old fences.

MANY VILLAGES AND TOWNS hold a cleanup day every year. Anyone can join in, including you. On this day, volunteers help to collect all the garbage lying around in the fields and forests. Wouldn't it be great if every day was cleanup day?

QUIZ

There is a huge garbage patch in the middle of the Pacific Ocean that contains tons of microplastics and all kinds of debris. How large is it?

* The size of Sydney, Australia
* The size of Nova Scotia, Canada
* Twice the size of Texas, USA

The patch is twice the size of Texas. Ocean currents trap debris from all over the world. Unfortunately, it is not the only patch of garbage floating in the ocean, but it is the largest.

Gray wolves, like dogs, love to play.

CHAPTER 6

ANIMAL LANGUAGE

ANIMALS HAVE A LOT TO SAY.
They do this with calls, and when they're feeling good, some animals can even laugh. But they also communicate with their bodies, to show what kind of mood they're in or what they want to do. If you look and listen closely, you too may be able to tell what animals are saying.

WHAT KINDS OF SOUNDS DO ANIMALS MAKE?

SQUAWK!

RIBBIT!

Of course, animals can't speak exactly the way we do. Only parrots can sometimes manage to say "human" words. But many species communicate in their own language. Take fish, for example.

WE ONCE THOUGHT THAT fish couldn't make sounds. Although fish constantly open and close their mouths to breathe, scientists have long overlooked (or, you could say, been deaf to) the fact that they also make sounds. Today we know that some fish can, for example, grind their teeth to communicate. Herring do something even more extraordinary. They fart to talk! A herring fart can last more than seven seconds. Researchers suspect that the fish use these sounds to find their way through their school. When herring fart like that, the other fish know where they are swimming. This is especially useful at night, when even fish can't see much.

*

For hundreds of years we've thought that horses simply neigh. But a few years ago, Swiss scientists discovered that they have a language if you listen carefully. We've known for a long time that a horse whinny can be high or low. But it turns out they can also do both at the same time, it's just that hardly anyone noticed. I've had horses for twenty years, and even I didn't realize this. They have different whinnies, depending on what they want to say.

*

Birdsong in spring is also a kind of language. Those beautiful melodies can be songs to attract mates, but they can also mean, "Get out of here. This spot is already taken!" In the fall the birds stop singing because they are no longer breeding and no longer need a territory. Then they talk using other sounds, such as peeping and croaking. They have a lot to tell each other. Siberian jays warn one another when a predator such as an owl or hawk is approaching. The jays have many different "words" for owl or hawk so that all members of their species know exactly which enemy is on its way.

An especially long, high whinny means "I don't like what's going on here!"

Prairie dogs also have quite a wide range of vocabulary to describe what kind of danger is approaching. The lookout can let the colony know if the danger is coming from the air or the ground, how fast it is approaching, how big it is, and even its color. The other prairie dogs then know what to look for and can take appropriate evasive action.

There are even different languages within the same species. For instance, I have little European robins at my forest lodge in Germany, but European robins also live in the Canary Islands in the Atlantic Ocean, far off the African coast. The robins there have very different calls than the ones who live near me. If one of my robins met one from Tenerife, they might not be able to understand one another.

Elephants also communicate with each other using sounds. The sounds of some "words" are so low that humans can't even hear them. They make a deep rumbling with their feet on the ground to warn other elephants. They also hear this rumbling through their feet and can find out this way, for example, whether lions are traveling nearby.

QUIZ

Even plants can talk. They do it with odors. Each smell means something different. How many such "plant words" have researchers discovered so far?

* 15
* 370
* 2,000

Researchers have so far discovered 2,000 "plant words," each one with a different smell.

TRY THIS!

IT'S A GOOD THING that animals talk so much! This way you can identify them without even seeing them. This works especially well with birds. Record a bird call with a cell phone. On the internet, you'll find websites that can help you identify birds based on their calls. If you find a match, you'll know which bird you heard singing.

Elephants also recognize each other through voice.

DO ANIMALS UNDERSTAND BODY LANGUAGE?

Humans speak without using words. Other people can tell by the look on your face whether you are sad, happy, or angry. They know immediately what's going on with you. Many animals communicate this way, too.

When a horse points its ears forward, it means it's listening to you.

HORSES LAY THEIR EARS back flat when they are in a bad mood. They also often beat their tails. When horses feel calm, they lower their heads and relax their ears.

*

Much body language is expressed with the head, especially the face. But you can also communicate with your whole body. If you're in a bad mood, you hold yourself differently than when you're in a good mood. Maybe you'll droop a bit or lower your head a little. Horses, for example, can see this immediately. They may not work as well with you then, because they know that someone who is in a bad mood is likely to be unfair. And horses do not like unfairness one bit.

*

Goats also observe the posture of humans closely. I see this every day in our pasture. Normally the goats come to me right away to be petted. But sometimes I have to trim their hooves. It's like cutting their fingernails—it doesn't hurt, but the goats don't like it. When I come to trim their hooves, they run away, even though I hide the clippers in my pocket. I try to act as normal as possible, but the goats are on to me right away. It's because your body posture changes just a bit when you are trying to look particularly inconspicuous.

*

Body language is often similar in animals and in humans. In soccer, watch a goalkeeper about to defend a penalty shot. What do you notice? Even dogs make themselves bigger when they want to impress a strange dog. They'll often raise their hackles and tail to make themselves look larger. On the other hand, if they're scared, they'll tuck their tail between their legs and make themselves small. Then a strange dog may not attack so quickly, because it doesn't feel threatened by a frightened dog.

*

Do you like it when a stranger looks into your eyes for a very long time? Definitely not, and cats and dogs consider it a threat, too. Strange cats stare at each other when one wants to chase the other away. And it is not a good idea to stare at an unfamiliar dog. It will think you want to attack it.

Eye contact can be pleasant, too. It feels nice when your parent or sibling gazes at you fondly. The same goes for the dogs in your family, who will know from your look that you are fond of them.

*

Other signals work very differently for humans and animals. For us, smiling is a sign that we are feeling friendly and relaxed. Sometimes you show your teeth when you smile. But for a dog, pulling back the lips and showing the teeth signals a threat.

TRY THIS!

CAN YOU COMMUNICATE WITH animals using body language? You don't need to have your own pets to find out. You can easily try this in a petting zoo, where the animals are used to humans. See if the animal guesses your intentions. Do you want to pet it? Do you want to feed it? Should it keep its distance? Behave the way you would with people and see if the animals understand you.

Look!

On Guard

CROWS TRY TO GUESS people's intentions from a distance. They want to know whether or not hunters are approaching. That's why crows check to see whether the human is carrying a rifle. If so, they will quickly fly away. They also flee from people with walking sticks, because the stick looks like a rifle to a crow.

Front end down low, back end up high means "Please play with me!"

DO ANIMALS HAVE A SENSE OF HUMOR?

Are there times when you just have to laugh? When you are being tickled, say, or when you do something funny? It's the same for some animals!

"Catch me if you can!" This seems to be what the cheeky hooded crow is saying to the dog.

FOR A LONG TIME people believed that animals couldn't laugh, even though some of them look as though they are smiling. In dolphins, the corners of the mouth are bent slightly upward. This is true whether they're in a good mood or a bad one. So you can't call that a smile. We also know that many animals are ticklish. Dogs, horses, or rats will laugh when you scratch their ticklish spots but the laugh doesn't sound like ours. Dogs pant, horses whinny, and you can't hear anything at all with rats. That's because their laugh is way too high for our ears to hear. Scientists have to use special microphones to hear the laughter of rats.

But do animals also laugh at jokes? Unfortunately, I don't know whether they tell jokes or not, because I don't really understand animal language. But there are animal species that do funny things, just for fun. For example, in the rain forest there are parrots who sit together in a tree. One of them pretends it can't fly. It just falls off the branch to the ground, while the other parrots screech with pleasure.

Some crows like to play tricks on dogs. They'll do this especially when the dog is tied up, perhaps in front of a store. When the dog isn't looking, the crow sneaks up, nips the dog's tail, and quickly jumps back a few steps. The dog of course turns around immediately and goes to chase the crow. But the dog is tied up, so it doesn't get far. The crow just stands there and finds it funny. And it is funny, because the dog forgot that it was on a leash and couldn't chase after the crow after all.

From time to time, though, a crow may annoy a dog that's not on a leash. Then it's time to fly off in a hurry!

Dogs can also make jokes, as in the case of two dogs who were playing with each other beside a pond. One of them simply pushed the other one into the water and thought it was great fun. The dog in the water probably didn't like it quite so much. You've probably played jokes like this with your friends.

Sometimes we humans also laugh out of relief, and animals can do the same thing. For instance, when a cat sneaks up on a bird's nest, the birds that notice become very excited. They try to scare or lure the cat away. The bird mother acts as though her own wing is broken, and she hops around in front of the cat. The cat thinks the bird is easy prey and tries to catch her. The mother bird keeps hopping farther and farther away, and when she has put enough distance between the cat and the nest, she'll fly back. The cat is gone, and the bird parents begin to chirp loudly in relief.

PEOPLE LAUGH WHEN THEY'RE tickled. But it's not just because your body parts are so sensitive. To get a ticklish feeling, someone else has to touch you—you can't tickle yourself. Try it and see if you feel anything other than a slight scratching feeling.

No one knows whether these dolphins are smiling, because they always look this friendly.

DO ANIMALS SHOW OFF?

Some people like to impress others with what they wear.
Animals do this too by showing off their fur or feathers.
It's as if they're saying, "Look at me! Don't I look fabulous!"

When the peacock fans his feathers, his tail looks like a big wheel with many eyes, and you just have to pay attention!

ANIMALS WANT TO DRAW particular attention to themselves during the mating season. Usually it's the males who like to look more beautiful, bigger, or more colorful than the others, so that the females will be especially attracted to them.

*

The peacock grows exceptionally long tail feathers for this very reason. Each feather has patterns that look like big eyes. The female birds are a dull gray-brown color, because they want to breed without being seen by other animals. They're on the lookout for the most beautiful male to start their family.

*

Male deer don't have feathers, but they do have antlers. Every year the male grows a new set on his head. The older and stronger the deer, the bigger the antlers. He wants to impress not just the female deer but especially the other males. When they see such a splendid set of antlers, they will decide to back off. Large antlers signal that he's a good fighter, but he'll only need to use them if another male won't give up without a battle. When all the other males are gone, the stag has the females to himself. Billy goats behave in much the same way. But they don't discard their two big horns, which stay on their heads for their whole lives.

*

The male alpine newt likes to impress females with his eye-catching colors. He knows they will want to mate with the most colorful fellow.

Alpine newts love the colors blue and orange. During mating season, the animals live in the water for several weeks. While the females tend to remain inconspicuous, the males turn blue with dark spots, while their bellies gleam bright orange. In the summer, the newts come out of the water again, and the bright colors fade.

＊

Sometimes animals show off certain parts of their bodies or certain colors not just to find a mate but to show rank. With roosters, for example, the size of the comb shows who is the strongest and most beautiful. With sparrows you have to look more closely. A large black patch on the breast and a dark beak are considered particularly impressive. The male sparrows don't just fight during mating season, but all year round. The beak of the strongest bird gets darker, and he grows a particularly large black breast patch. So everyone knows right away who's the boss.

Look!

All Puffed Up

HUMANS SOMETIMES IMITATE ANIMALS. If you want to look important, make yourself big and beautiful. You can see this with the guards in front of Buckingham Palace in London, UK. They want to impress their audience, so they wear tall bearskin caps. They also wear dashing bright red tunics that draw everybody's attention.

QUIZ

About how many feathers does the tundra swan have?

＊ 1,300

＊ 15,000

＊ 25,000

The tundra swan has 25,000 feathers and holds the record among birds. A sparrow, for example, only has about 1,300 feathers.

Even dogs and cats can be best friends.

CHAPTER 7

ANIMAL EMOTIONS

DOGS ARE HAPPY WHEN THEY meet their friends, and flies can experience fear. Animals have feelings that are familiar to us. And because dogs, crows, and whales know that it's no fun feeling scared, sometimes they even help other animals. This can sometimes take courage!

DO ANIMALS EVER FEEL SCARED?

Being afraid is not a good feeling. Everybody knows that. But fear is also important in life. Those who don't feel fear live very dangerously, and it's the same for animals.

A roadrunner sprints across a road.

IS THERE SOMETHING YOU'RE scared of? If so, then you are completely normal. For example, if you stand on the edge of a steep bank, you're afraid of falling off. This fear is innate, and it protects you so that you don't put yourself in danger.

Animals know these fears, too. They also stay back from the edge of a cliff so they don't fall off.

Animals learn many fears only during the course of their lives. When a fox mother gets a fright, her children become frightened, too. They have no idea why, at first. Perhaps the fox mother is frightened because she has seen a human. Foxes are sometimes hunted, so humans can be dangerous predators for them. The fox children see that their mother is frightened, and they learn that humans are to be feared and that it's best to run away from them. In areas where foxes are commonly hunted, being afraid of humans is an important thing for fox children to know. They'll survive much longer that way. But shooting isn't allowed in the city, so here foxes learn that humans are not dangerous.

＊

Animals can set aside their fear, the same way we do. But doing so can take time, because fear can be very strong. You may know that from your experiences with spiders. Although most of the ones that live near us are not dangerous (unless you live in Australia), many people are still afraid of them. Even when they learn that the spiders are completely harmless, they may remain afraid of them for their whole lives.

＊

Foxes, wild boars, dogs, or cats are similar to us because we are closely related. It's easy to understand that they can be afraid. But what about animals that are very different from us?

＊

Researchers have long thought that fish did not feel fear. The fish have nothing at the spot deep in the brain where fear is produced in humans. But then scientists found that a fish's fear center is at the top of the brain. They probably could just have asked anglers, who know that fish understand the danger perfectly. A fish that has been on the hook and been released is not so quick to bite a hook again. It's afraid of being pulled out of the water. It hurts, for one thing, and once it's out of the water, the fish can no longer breathe.

＊

At home it's easy to get a close-up look at how fear works. Even flies can be afraid! Maybe you've tried to catch one by hand. The first time you try, you may get close, but even by the second time it is more difficult. The fly now knows that your hand is dangerous, and it is afraid. That's why it flies off a little sooner.

A mother bear teaches her cubs to escape danger by climbing up the nearest tree.

TRY THIS!

PAY ATTENTION TO YOUR feelings when you play tag or hide-and-seek with your friends. You know that nothing bad is going to happen and that in fact playing the game is fun. And yet, when someone sneaks up to your hiding place or is just about to catch you, you feel a bit scared. But because you're playing a game, the tingling in your belly is exciting and it feels nice. So a little dose of fear can be fun!

ARE ANIMALS BRAVE?

Fear and courage go together, even in the animal world. Courage means being afraid and overcoming the fear. This is sometimes easier to do when you're with others. I'd like to tell you about some animals that live near me in Germany.

Fieldfares are native to Europe and Asia.

FIELDFARES ARE BIRDS ABOUT the size of American robins. They build their nests in trees. As a rule, they are very scared of crows, which are much bigger and stronger and will usually win any fight. Usually. Because when the fieldfare builds its nest and lays eggs, it becomes courageous. Crows love those eggs, and sometimes they will try to steal them. The fieldfares don't like this. Although they are much weaker, they will dive-bomb the crow. And because this works better as a group, a number of birds will get together and swarm the crow and attack together. They can't hurt the crow, but they will annoy the black bird until it finally flies away. Their courage is especially effective because they work together.

*

But even individual animals can be courageous, I've seen this myself in the forest. My dog Maxi was supposed to drive a doe and her fawn out of an enclosure that the two had wandered into. As Maxi chased them, the doe quickly ran away with her fawn. But even as the mother ran toward the exit, the fawn decided to put a stop to things. It suddenly turned and ran at Maxi. The dog was so shocked that she turned tail and fled. A fawn attacking a dog? It was such a surprise to Maxi that she got scared and ran.

*

Courage often comes from love. Mothers defend their children, even when they would rather run away. It's like this with many animals.

But what about those who are not so brave? Do they have a worse time in life because they never really defend themselves, but instead just make a run for it?

*

If you're going to be brave, it's good idea to know what's out there.

Researchers have found that anxious animals can also have an advantage. This has been observed in the bird species, great tits. The bravest birds quickly snatch up the best goodies while the more timid ones prefer to wait and check out their surroundings. There might be a dangerous cat nearby, so the cautious birds will keep looking around instead of flying straight to the food. And other shy birds will often do the same.

*

Scientists have observed that these not-so-courageous great tits don't like being in large groups where the birds make a lot of noise and constantly fly back and forth. It's all too much for the careful, reserved tits. They like to band together in small groups, preferably with other tits that tend to be anxious as well. In these small groups the tits don't like to quarrel, so they rarely do. Instead, they take their time before they finally decide to take action.

This doesn't mean the brave tits have eaten everything. Flying around and pecking in a hurry means overlooking many things. The shyer birds may discover seeds from the previous summer, which are harder to see in the bushes. So in the end, they will find just as much food as the brave birds.

TRY THIS!

WANT TO UNDERSTAND WHAT it's like to be a timid tit? If so, try the following test. Take a notebook and a pen and sit outside. See how many animals you can spot in the first few seconds. Write down the result.

Now keep an eye on your surroundings for at least ten minutes. How many animals can you count this time (count every one, whether it's a bird, beetle, or cat)? Look down as well. You may see little bugs and spiders that are easy to overlook. Note this result, and you'll see for yourself that taking your time means discovering much more.

In small groups, tits don't like to argue, and so they hardly ever do.

DO ANIMALS LOOK OUT FOR EACH OTHER?

Animals living in families help one another—when hunting, for example. But what about different species? Do they help each other out, too?

Even whales find baby animals cute. Maybe the seal in the story below reminded the helpful humpback of a young whale.

CATS SOMETIMES CATCH BIRDS in the garden. This is obviously why birds don't like cats, right? If a cat is in trouble, the birds should be happy, because they will be in less danger themselves.

But in at least one case things didn't happen this way. A crow lived in the garden belonging to an elderly couple. They called the crow Moses. One day a little kitten came into the garden. It clearly had no parents and was already half starved. But Moses looked for earthworms and beetles and began to feed the kitten. It survived, and the friendship between the crow and the cat lasted for many years.

*

Such helpfulness can be found again and again in nature, including in whales. Scientists have observed a humpback whale protecting a seal. The seal was being hunted by orca whales that wanted to eat it. The much larger humpback kept pushing itself between the orcas and the seal and even lifted the seal up on its fin. The orcas couldn't get to it, and they finally gave up.

*

Why would animals do such things? After all, a crow can't care much about the fate of a kitten, and humpback whales usually have nothing to do with seals. Humans are moved to help others through a feeling of compassion. If someone is in danger or isn't feeling well, we empathize with them and want to help. This seems to be true of some animals, too. Your dog may try to comfort you if you are feeling bad. They lean in close, lick your hands or face, and sometimes howl a little.

*

In Berlin there was once a dog who took care of small wild boars. The mother of the piglets was dead, and they were almost frozen. Passersby found them and took them to an animal shelter, where a dog adopted the small boars and took care of them until they were grown. Similar examples can be seen again and again. Sometimes dogs will raise kittens or another dog's puppies.

*

In some animals, helping friends of their own species seems to be common. A bat species in South America is known for sharing food. If a bat has bad luck and can't find anything to eat, the others will give it something when they come back to the cave. Then nobody has to go hungry. The bat who receives the food remembers who gave it to them. If the helper goes hungry another time, this time it will get food as thanks.

*

Can animals really be thankful? I'm pretty sure they can. Cats and dogs in shelters are often very anxious. They think nobody wants them. When a person comes to take them in, they show how happy they are.

    I once experienced this myself with an old cocker spaniel. His name was Barry and he was already nine years old when we adopted him. He loved being home with us but hated traveling in the car. Maybe he was afraid that if he got into the car, he would be given away again.

TRY THIS!

THOUSANDS OF DOGS AND cats are placed in shelters each year. They are given away because their owners no longer want them or can't take care of them anymore. If you and your family would like a pet, it's a good idea not to buy it, but to visit a shelter. Maybe you'll find a dog, a cat, a couple of guinea pigs, or a rabbit that you like. You can then give these animals a new home.

DO ANIMALS DREAM?

When you sleep, you often dream. Maybe you don't always realize this because you don't remember all your dreams the next morning. But what about animals? Can they dream, too?

Horses like this foal only lie down when they feel safe.

HAVE YOU EVER WATCHED a dog in a deep sleep? Sometimes it will start to bark in its sleep and its paws will twitch. The dog is dreaming, perhaps about chasing a rabbit. Maybe you've seen a similar thing with cats, too, but have you ever seen a horse dream? Although they only sleep soundly for a few minutes at a time, they often lie on their sides and move their hooves in the air.

In a dream you can experience many things—sometimes even things that aren't possible in real life.

For example, I have had dreams that I could fly. In my dream state, all I had to do was move my arms up and down.

*

But how do we know that animals really dream, and what they dream about? Researchers have tested rats. There is an instrument that can measure the brain waves of animals. A rat's brain works just like ours electrically. It consists of many pathways through which currents flow during thinking and dreaming. You can measure these brain waves and look at the results on a computer screen.

First the researchers put the rats in a maze. The instrument measured the brain waves depending on where the animals were in the maze. At night, researchers measured the brain waves while the rats slept. Based on the patterns on the screen, they could see that the rats were dreaming of the maze, and they could even tell exactly where they were in it in their dreams!

*

There's another clue that animals truly dream. When people dream, their eyes will move around wildly. Maybe you can check this out yourself if your mom or dad falls asleep on the couch. Watch their eyelids to see whether their eyes are moving rapidly underneath. This only happens now and then—you don't dream the whole time you are sleeping. It's the same with many animals. Dogs, cats, horses, or even birds—they all roll their eyes from time to time in their sleep.

*

But what about very small animals? Flies and other insects don't have eyelids, so they can't even close their eyes. Nevertheless, they do sleep, and even with tiny animals, researchers can observe what we already know from watching larger animals—they kick their legs.

*

Why are sleep and dreams so important? Researchers don't know the whole answer, but one thing is certain. The brain needs to rest at night. Only then does it really store what it has learned during the day. And animals learn a lot every day!

However, there are also quite a few animals that never sleep at night. Bats and many moths, but also owls and foxes are active during this time. But because they get tired just as we do, they just dream during the day instead.

Sweet dreams, little owl!

TRY THIS!

IF YOU NEED TO study something for school, try reading the important things in the evening. Your brain will work especially hard at night, and you will probably remember what you've learned better.

Koalas have extra padding on their bottoms so they can curl up comfortably as they sleep in trees, which is important because they sleep up to eighteen hours a day!

PHOTO CREDITS

2 left muddy hands © Sasiistock / iStockphoto.com; **right** butterfly © ballycroy / iStockphoto.com

3 top and bottom Peter Wohlleben, portrait © Jens Steingässer

4–5 children at nature reserve © Image Source / iStockphoto.com

6 slugs © Lisa S / Shutterstock.com

7 left butterflies © KatieDobies / iStockphoto.com; **top right** forget-me-nots © Fire-fly / Shutterstock.com; **bottom right** stones © Jens Steingässer

8 robins © MelodyanneM / iStockphoto.com

9 left Canada Geese © RCKeller / iStockphoto.com; **right** hummingbird nest © Terryfic3D / iStockphoto.com

10 wolf pup © Geoffrey Kuchera / Shutterstock.com

11 hoof print © Jens Steingässer

12 top stonefly nymph © 23frogger / Shutterstock.com; **middle** tadpoles © Savo Ilic / Shutterstock.com

13 left common merganser © Anna39 / iStockphoto.com; **right** girl with glass jar © Antonia Banyard

14–15 barn swallows © Olexandr Panchenko / Shutterstock.com

16 beech-leaf miners © Jens Steingässer

17 left fox mother and kits © Jukka Jantunen / Shutterstock.com; **right** pygmy shrew © Rudmer Zwerver / Shutterstock.com

18 deer © gsagi / iStockphoto.com

19 left flowers © Jens Steingässer; **right** long-horned beetle © Henrik Larsson / Shutterstock.com

20 burying beetle © Anatolich / Shutterstock.com

21 left deer droppings © Jens Steingässer; **right** rabbit and dung © Atovot / Shutterstock.com

22 top hare © Volodymyr Burdiak / Shutterstock.com; **middle** moth © Rosemarie Kappler / Shutterstock.com

23 left caterpillar © Marek R. Swadzba / Shutterstock.com; **right** puffer fish © Aleksei Alekhin / Shutterstock.com

24–25 frog © Marco Maggesi / Shutterstock.com

26 midwife toad © Hector Ruiz Villar / Shutterstock.com

27 left salamander larvae © Dieter Herrmann / Shutterstock.com; **right** wood pile © Jens Steingässer

28 left butterfly © Bildagentur Zoonar GmbH / Shutterstock.com; **right** oak gall © D. Kucharski K. Kucharska / Shutterstock.com

29 top wolf spider © Peter Yeeles / Shutterstock.com; **bottom** monarch caterpillar © CathyKeifer / iStockphoto.com

30 emu © TonyBaggett / iStockphoto.com

31 top robin's nest © phi2 / iStockphoto.com; **bottom** chick © Donna A. Herrmann / Shutterstock.com

32 horses © Bildagentur Zoonar GmbH / Shutterstock.com

33 top platypus © John Carnemolla / Shutterstock.com; **bottom** nursing bear © USO / iStockphoto.com

34–35 opossums © Evelyn D. Harrison / Shutterstock.com

36 minnows © Jan phanomphrai / Shutterstock.com

37 left ladybugs © andibern / iStockphoto.com; **right** stick insect © crbellette / iStockphoto.com

INDEX

HOW TO USE THIS INDEX

This book discusses many facts and topics about animals, like which animals you can find in your backyard, and how animals laugh and dream. This index will help you quickly find these facts by telling you what pages the facts are on.

To use the index, find the topic you are interested in. The topics are in alphabetical order. The numbers after each topic are the page numbers that you can use to find the information. Page numbers in a range (as in 6–7) means that information is found on both pages 6 and 7. Page numbers in bold indicate something special on the page, like a picture, quiz, or activity. Sometimes similar information is listed under a different topic. You can find these if you see the words *See* or *See also*, and follow the cross-reference to the new topic.

Text copyright © 2019 by Peter Wohlleben
Originally published in German as *Weißt du, wo die Tiere wohnen.*
Eine Entdeckungsreise durch Wiese und Wald © 2019
Verlag Friedrich Oetinger, Hamburg
English translation copyright © 2021 by Shelley Tanaka

First published in Canada, the U.S., and the U.K. by Greystone Books in 2021

21 22 23 24 25   5 4 3 2 1

Greystone Kids / Greystone Books Ltd.
greystonebooks.com

Cataloguing data available from Library and Archives Canada
ISBN 978-1-77164-659-8 (cloth)
ISBN 978-1-77164-660-4 (epub)

The publisher wishes to thank Dr. Cora Skaien
for her valuable contribution in reviewing the book.

Editing by Jane Billinghurst
Copy editing by Eleanor Rose
Proofreading by Alison Strobel
Indexing by Stephen Ullstrom
Jacket, interior design, and illustrations by Belle Wuthrich
Jacket photo © stanley45 / iStockphoto.com
Photo selection for the English edition by Antonia Banyard

Printed and bound in Malaysia on ancient-forest-friendly paper by Tien Wah Press

Greystone Books gratefully acknowledges the Musqueam, Squamish,
and Tsleil-Waututh peoples on whose land our office is located.

Greystone Books thanks the Canada Council for the Arts, the British Columbia Arts
Council, the Province of British Columbia through the Book Publishing Tax Credit, and the
Government of Canada for supporting our publishing activities.